THE FINANCIAL ARK PHILOSOPHY FOR BLACK INDEPENDENCE

Copyright © 2024 by author **Kevin Barron**

No part of this publication may be reproduced, distributed, or transmitted in any form or by any means, or stored in any database or retrieval system, without prior written permission of the publisher **BLACK RISING LLC.**

Disclaimer

I am not an expert, advisor, or consultant in finance, business, real estate, or any other field discussed in this material. The information, opinions, and philosophies shared here are my personal views and are meant for informational and educational purposes only. They should not be taken as professional advice or guidance.

It is important to do your own research, consult with licensed professionals, and thoroughly investigate the topics mentioned before making any financial, business, or investment decisions. Every individual's situation is unique, and what works for one person may not be suitable for another. Therefore, I strongly encourage you to seek advice from qualified experts in the relevant fields to ensure that any action you take is well-informed and tailored to your specific circumstances.

Other books by Kevin Barron

Fiction

Black Rising

Black Rising: Home and Abroad

Black Rising: The Threat

Collateral Consequences

Non-fiction

Summary Introduction to the Books of the Bible

Applied Christianity Handbook

The Financial Ark Philosophy for Black Independence

The *Financial Ark Philosophy* is based on the belief that true independence, power, and freedom for Black people can only be achieved through economic self-sufficiency. Just as Noah's Ark was constructed to save humanity from a coming flood, the Financial Ark Philosophy is designed to safeguard Black communities from the economic storms of inequality, systemic disenfranchisement, and financial instability. This "Ark" is a vessel built to carry Black people to a future of empowerment, where they are no longer dependent on external systems that have historically marginalized them.

The Financial Ark Philosophy is not merely about survival; it's about thriving in a world that has often excluded Black people from the full benefits of wealth. Its mission is to foster financial literacy, entrepreneurial spirit, and collective ownership within the Black community. By embracing these four pillars, business, stocks, real estate, and God, this philosophy prepares Black people for economic storms, while creating a future where they can flourish on their own terms. Much like Noah's Ark, which was built in anticipation of a coming flood, the Financial Ark Philosophy is a proactive, forward-thinking initiative designed to protect Black communities from future crises. Its goal is to guide Black people away from the metaphorical floodwaters of financial inequality and toward the shores of independence, security, and power. In the Ark, the journey is not just about individual success. it's about collective progress, bringing the entire community aboard and sailing toward a shared destiny of financial freedom.

Four Pillars of the Ark

1. Starting a Business

The first pillar of the Financial Ark Philosophy. By creating Black-owned businesses, individuals gain control over their livelihoods and communities. Entrepreneurship allows Black people to break free from the limitations of traditional employment structures, where they are often underrepresented or exploited. Businesses generate wealth, provide jobs, and build the foundation of a self-sustaining economy. Every business is a building block in the Ark, ensuring that Black communities are not reliant on outside entities for economic survival.

2. Investing in the Stock Market

The second pillar is stock market investment, representing the Ark's ability to float above the tides of capitalism. By learning to navigate the financial markets, Black people can become shareholders in the global economy, growing wealth and accessing opportunities that were once inaccessible. Investing in stocks gives individuals part ownership of some of the largest corporations in America, shifting Black people from consumers to stakeholders. This participation in the financial system helps to close the racial wealth gap and equips future generations with the knowledge and resources to stay afloat in any economic climate.

3. Investing in Real Estate

The third pillar of the Financial Ark Philosophy is real estate investment. Land and property ownership forms the solid ground upon which generational wealth is built. By investing in real estate, Black people can secure assets that appreciate over time, provide housing stability, and offer a source of passive income. Real estate represents the Ark's anchor, ensuring that Black communities have both physical and economic roots in the land.

4. God

The fourth pillar of the Financial Ark Philosophy is **The Pillar of God**, which acknowledges that true wealth and prosperity come from a foundation grounded in faith, ethics, and alignment with God's principles. While starting a business, investing in the stock market, and real estate are powerful tools for financial independence, wealth is incomplete without spiritual guidance. The Bible offers timeless wisdom on wealth, money, and prosperity, framing financial success as a tool for fulfilling God's purpose in our lives and helping others.

Section One

The First Pillar of the Financial Ark Philosophy: Starting a Business

Starting a business is the foundational step in building the *Financial Ark,* creating an economic and financial system aimed at achieving true independence, power, and freedom for Black people through economic self-sufficiency. Let us briefly explore how creating Black-owned businesses allows individuals to take control of their own economic destiny, breaking away from the limitations and systemic obstacles of traditional employment structures. The mission of starting Black-owned businesses isn't just about individual success; it's about fostering a network of self-sustaining enterprises that uplift entire communities.

A Historical Perspective: Why Entrepreneurship Matters for Black Communities

For centuries, Black people have faced structural barriers to economic participation. From slavery and segregation to redlining and systemic discrimination in the job market, Black people have been systematically excluded from mainstream economic opportunities. Entrepreneurship is a powerful antidote to these historical inequalities. Starting a business enables Black individuals to bypass the gatekeepers of traditional employment, who have often denied them access to fair wages, promotions, or even basic job opportunities.

In the era of Jim Crow laws, Black communities created *"parallel economies,"* where Black-owned businesses thrived despite the oppressive legal and social structures that sought to marginalize them. One of the most famous examples is the Greenwood District in Tulsa, Oklahoma, popularly known as "Black Wall Street." During the early 20th century, Black Wall Street was a bustling hub of Black-owned businesses that thrived despite the larger society's segregation and racism. This community of entrepreneurs created a self-sufficient economy where Black residents could find employment, access goods and services, and accumulate wealth.

The success of Black Wall Street and similar enclaves across the country proves that Black entrepreneurship can serve as a vehicle for both economic survival and prosperity. However, these communities were often targeted, with the Tulsa massacre of 1921 being a devastating reminder of how systemic racism works to undermine Black success. Even so, these historical examples highlight that entrepreneurship has always been a necessary path toward economic freedom for Black people. It also demonstrated that we must learn to protect our accomplishments, our people, and our successes.

Today, starting a business remains one of the most powerful ways to reclaim control over our economic destiny, especially in a world where wage gaps, hiring discrimination, and lack of access to leadership positions remain rampant.

Control Over Livelihoods

One of the most immediate benefits of starting a business is the control it offers over your own livelihood. In a traditional job, many Black employees are subject to external decision-makers who may not understand, respect, or prioritize their unique needs and talents. Systemic racism manifests itself in the workplace through biased hiring practices, wage disparities, and limited opportunities for advancement. A Black entrepreneur, however, is free to carve out a space that aligns with their own values, community needs, and personal ambitions.

Entrepreneurship also allows individuals to decide their working conditions. Instead of being subject to the structural inequalities of predominantly white corporate environments, Black business owners can create workspaces that are culturally affirming and supportive of diversity. Whether it's flexible work hours, equitable pay structures, or providing services and products that resonate with the Black community, entrepreneurship enables autonomy and freedom from the limitations imposed by others.

The autonomy gained through entrepreneurship goes beyond the day-to-day operations of the business. Black entrepreneurs have the ability to choose the direction of their ventures, identify market opportunities, and scale in ways that are beneficial to their long-term vision. This control over one's economic path empowers individuals to build wealth that can be passed down through generations.

Job Creation and Community Empowerment

Starting a business doesn't just empower the individual entrepreneur; it empowers the entire community. In predominantly Black neighborhoods, unemployment and underemployment are often disproportionately high due to systemic barriers. By creating Black-owned businesses, entrepreneurs can generate jobs for their community members, providing employment opportunities that are otherwise scarce. This type of job creation not only reduces unemployment but also helps stabilize families, improve education outcomes for children, and decrease crime rates in economically depressed areas.

Additionally, Black-owned businesses can serve as role models for younger generations. By highlighting successful Black entrepreneurs, communities can instill a sense of pride, motivation, and possibility among youth who might otherwise feel disconnected from the mainstream economy. The narrative shifts from one of exclusion to one of ownership.

When young Black people see others who look like them running successful businesses, it breaks down the psychological barriers to what they believe is possible for their own futures.

Moreover, Black entrepreneurs are uniquely positioned to provide products and services tailored to the needs of the Black community, filling gaps in the marketplace that are often ignored by mainstream corporations. Whether it is hair care products for Black consumers, culturally relevant media, or financial services that address the specific needs of Black families, Black-owned businesses can create offerings that resonate deeply with their target demographic. These businesses not only cater to an underserved market but also foster a sense of pride and identity within the community.

Building the Foundation of a Self-Sustaining Economy

At the core of the Financial Ark Philosophy is the idea of building a self-sustaining economy. This goes beyond individual businesses to create an ecosystem of enterprises that work together to provide for the community's needs. Historically, Black communities have been disproportionately dependent on external economic structures that are not designed to serve their best interests. This dependency has left Black people vulnerable to exploitation, economic downturns, and systemic neglect. By creating a network of Black-owned businesses, the community can begin to generate wealth from within, reducing reliance on outside corporations or institutions that often prioritize profit over people.

A self-sustaining economy requires more than just isolated businesses; it demands interconnectedness. This means Black-owned businesses buying from one another, circulating money within the community, and supporting each other's growth. For example, a Black-owned construction company can source materials from a Black-owned supplier, while a Black-owned restaurant can hire local farmers for their produce. This type of economic interdependence keeps money circulating within the community, fostering ***collective prosperity***.

In addition to creating a self-sustaining economy, entrepreneurship also helps build generational wealth. Unlike traditional employment, where wages typically stop at the end of the pay period, business ownership provides the potential for long-term wealth accumulation. Businesses can be sold, passed down, or expanded, creating opportunities for the next generation to inherit not only financial assets but also the knowledge and experience of running a successful enterprise.

Building a network of Black-owned businesses also helps insulate the community from external economic shocks. During recessions or economic downturns, Black communities are often hit the hardest because they lack control over the industries or corporations that dominate the job market. A self-sustaining economy, anchored by Black entrepreneurship, provides a buffer against these external forces. Even in times of economic uncertainty, Black-owned businesses can continue to serve the needs of their communities, ensuring that the essential goods and services remain accessible.

Overcoming Barriers to Entrepreneurship

While the benefits of starting a business are clear, it is important to recognize the unique challenges that Black entrepreneurs face. Systemic racism and discrimination have historically limited access to the resources needed to start and grow businesses. For instance, Black entrepreneurs often struggle to secure financing, as banks and investors are less likely to lend to Black-owned businesses. This lack of access to capital is one of the most significant barriers to entrepreneurship in the Black community.

Addressing these challenges requires a multi-faceted approach. One solution is the creation of Black-led financial institutions, venture capital firms, and angel investors who prioritize investing in Black-owned businesses. Another is the development of community-based crowdfunding platforms, where individuals can pool their resources to support local entrepreneurs. Additionally, mentorship programs can connect aspiring Black entrepreneurs with experienced business owners who can offer guidance, advice, and support throughout the startup process.

Moreover, Black entrepreneurs must advocate for policy changes that level the playing field. This includes pushing for reforms that address discriminatory lending practices, increasing government grants and subsidies for minority-owned businesses, and expanding access to business education and training programs.

The Importance of Financial Literacy and Business Education

A crucial component of successful entrepreneurship is financial literacy. Too often, Black entrepreneurs are not given the tools or education necessary to manage the financial aspects of their businesses effectively. This lack of knowledge can lead to mismanagement, debt, or even business failure. For the *Financial Ark* to thrive, there must be a concerted effort to teach financial literacy and business acumen within the Black community.

This can be achieved through community workshops, online courses, and mentorship programs focused on teaching the fundamentals of entrepreneurship, such as accounting, marketing, sales, and management. By equipping aspiring business owners with the knowledge, they need to succeed, the community can create a generation of entrepreneurs who are well-prepared to navigate the complexities of the business world.

Financial literacy also extends beyond the individual entrepreneur to the broader community. If Black consumers understand the importance of supporting Black-owned businesses and circulating wealth within their own community, they can become a powerful force for economic change. This type of collective financial consciousness is essential for building a self-sustaining economy.

The Long-Term Vision: Economic Sovereignty

Starting a business is not just about creating wealth; it's about reclaiming power. Economic independence is a critical component of political and social freedom. When Black communities control their own businesses, they also gain the power to influence policy, advocate for their rights, and resist the systems that have historically oppressed them. Economic sovereignty means that Black people can no longer be coerced, exploited, or marginalized by external forces. They are in control of their own future.

Entrepreneurship as a Vehicle for Community Empowerment

Starting a business is not merely an individual endeavor; it is a community effort that can uplift an entire group of people. Black entrepreneurship, in particular, has always had a social component, with businesses serving as more than just profit-driven enterprises. Historically, Black-owned businesses have been safe havens for cultural expression, political discourse, and community organization. From barbershops and salons to bookstores and restaurants, Black businesses have often been community hubs where people gather to discuss issues affecting their lives, share information, and organize for social and political change.

In the context of the *Financial Ark*, Black-owned businesses function as vessels that carry not just economic opportunity but also social cohesion and political power. These businesses can help address systemic inequalities by providing services, jobs, and a sense of agency to those who have been marginalized. In communities where traditional institutions like banks, grocery stores, and healthcare providers are often absent or inadequate, Black-owned businesses step in to fill the void.

Moreover, entrepreneurship provides the opportunity to challenge and redefine the narrative of Black economic participation. By starting businesses that focus on solving problems within their communities, Black entrepreneurs can reshape their local economies in ways that better serve their needs. For example, businesses that focus on healthy food options in food deserts, community-based financial services, or education resources tailored to underserved Black students contribute to a stronger and more resilient community.

This level of community empowerment is integral to the *Financial Ark* because it demonstrates that economic success and social progress can and must go hand in hand. When Black entrepreneurs succeed, they have the power to reinvest in their communities, creating a ripple effect that leads to long-term, sustainable progress.

Scaling and Expanding Black-Owned Businesses

While starting a business is a powerful first step, scaling that business to reach its full potential is the next challenge. Black entrepreneurs often face significant hurdles when it comes to expanding their businesses, such as limited access to capital, resources, and networks. In fact, many Black-owned businesses are often forced to operate as small, family-run enterprises due to these constraints, limiting their ability to scale, innovate, and compete in larger markets.

Scaling a business requires not just financial investment but also strategic planning, market expansion, and operational efficiency. For Black entrepreneurs to fully realize the potential of their enterprises, they need access to mentorship, training, and capital investment. Organizations and initiatives that focus on supporting Black businesses at this stage can play a crucial role in helping entrepreneurs overcome these obstacles. By offering mentorship, access to industry networks, and funding opportunities, these organizations enable Black-owned businesses to grow beyond their immediate communities and tap into regional, national, and even global markets.

Furthermore, scaling Black-owned businesses is essential for breaking into industries where Black people have historically been underrepresented, such as technology, manufacturing, and international trade. By expanding into these sectors, Black entrepreneurs can diversify their revenue streams, increase their influence, and create more high-paying jobs for their communities.

Scaling also allows Black businesses to move from being simply local service providers to industry leaders and innovators. For example, a Black-owned technology startup that begins by offering IT services to local clients can scale into developing proprietary software or providing cutting-edge technological solutions to major corporations. This kind of scaling not only generates significant wealth for the business owner but also positions the company as a leader in the broader economy.

By building and scaling Black-owned businesses, the *Financial Ark* creates pathways for economic diversification within Black communities. This diversification is essential for long-term sustainability because it reduces dependency on any single sector or industry, making the community more resilient to economic shifts and downturns.

The Role of Technology in Black Entrepreneurship

Technology has revolutionized the way businesses are started, operated, and scaled, providing Black entrepreneurs with unprecedented opportunities to enter industries that were previously inaccessible. In the context of the *Financial Ark*, technology is a powerful tool that can accelerate the creation of Black-owned businesses and broaden their impact.

The rise of e-commerce platforms, social media, and digital marketing has significantly lowered the barriers to entry for new businesses. Entrepreneurs no longer need to rely on physical storefronts, large advertising budgets, or even traditional banking systems to start and grow a business. With the internet and digital tools, a Black entrepreneur can launch a business from their living room, reach customers across the globe, and build a brand using free or low-cost platforms.

For example, Black-owned beauty brands have exploded in recent years, thanks in part to social media platforms like Instagram and YouTube, where entrepreneurs can display their products, engage directly with consumers, and build loyal followings. By leveraging these digital tools, many Black-owned businesses have been able to bypass traditional gatekeepers, such as retail stores or advertising agencies, and build direct-to-consumer models that have proven to be highly successful.

Moreover, technology allows Black entrepreneurs to innovate in ways that are uniquely tailored to the needs of their communities. Mobile apps, online platforms, and digital services can address gaps in healthcare, education, financial services, and more. For example, Black-owned fintech companies are developing platforms that provide financial services to underbanked communities, while Black-owned tech startups are creating educational tools that focus on Black history and culture. In this way, technology serves as both an equalizer and an amplifier for Black entrepreneurship, making it easier to start businesses, reach customers, and scale operations.

However, it's important to acknowledge that access to technology and digital infrastructure is not always equitable. The digital divide—where certain communities lack access to reliable internet, digital literacy, and technological tools can disproportionately affect Black entrepreneurs, especially those in underserved areas. To fully realize the potential of technology in the *Financial Ark*, efforts must be made to close this digital divide through investments in broadband access, technology training, and digital literacy programs.

Collective Ownership Models: Cooperatives and Collective Enterprises

One of the most exciting ways in which the *Financial Ark* can help foster economic independence is through the promotion of collective ownership models. In traditional business structures, wealth is concentrated in the hands of a single owner or a small group of shareholders. However, in collective ownership models, such as cooperatives or collective enterprises, the business is owned and managed by the workers or the community itself. This model is especially relevant for Black communities, where collective economic empowerment has always been a central goal.

Worker-owned cooperatives, for example, are businesses that are owned and operated by their employees. Each worker has an equal share in the business and a say in decision-making, which promotes economic equity and shared prosperity. This model has been particularly successful in industries like agriculture, retail, and food services, where workers are often underpaid and undervalued in traditional corporate structures. By sharing ownership and profits, worker cooperatives can help reduce income inequality and ensure that wealth is distributed more fairly within the community.

Collective ownership models also provide a solution to one of the most persistent problems facing Black entrepreneurs: access to capital. In a cooperative model, the financial burden of starting and maintaining a business is spread across multiple owners, which reduces the risks for any single individual. Additionally, cooperatives often receive support from community-based lending institutions, grant programs, and government initiatives aimed at promoting economic inclusion.

For example, a Black-owned grocery store in an underserved neighborhood could be structured as a cooperative, where community members pool their resources to start the business and share in its profits. This not only creates jobs and provides essential services to the community but also ensures that the wealth generated by the business stays within the community.

By promoting collective ownership models as part of the *Financial Ark*, Black communities can build businesses that are more resilient, equitable, and sustainable. These models encourage collaboration, reduce individual risk, and create opportunities for shared prosperity.

Policy Advocacy and Government Support for Black Entrepreneurship

While individual and community-driven efforts are essential for the success of the *Financial Ark*, systemic change is also necessary to create a more equitable environment for Black entrepreneurs. Policy advocacy plays a crucial role in dismantling the barriers that Black business owners face, from discriminatory lending practices to inequitable access to government contracts.

For example, government programs that offer grants, low-interest loans, or tax incentives for minority-owned businesses can provide much-needed financial support to Black entrepreneurs. Additionally, policies that promote supplier diversity require government agencies and large corporations to source a percentage of their goods and services from minority-owned businesses can open new markets for Black entrepreneurs.

Moreover, local governments can play a role in supporting Black-owned businesses by investing in infrastructure, creating business incubators, and providing technical assistance. For example, city governments can create commercial districts that are specifically designed to support Black-owned businesses, offering affordable rent, tax incentives, and access to resources like business mentorship and legal assistance.

Advocating for these types of policy changes is essential for long-term success. While entrepreneurship is a powerful tool for economic empowerment, it cannot exist in a vacuum. The broader systemic barriers that have historically excluded Black people from economic participation must be addressed in order to create a truly equitable and inclusive economy.

Measuring Success: Beyond Profits

For the *Financial Ark* to fulfill its mission, success must be measured in more than just profits. While financial success is important, the real impact of Black entrepreneurship lies in its ability to create lasting social, economic, and political change. This means that the success of the *Financial Ark* should be determined by how many jobs are created, how much wealth is generated and retained within Black communities, and how entrepreneurship contributes to broader goals of social justice and equity.

One way to measure success is by tracking the economic impact of Black-owned businesses on their local communities. This includes metrics such as the number of jobs created, the amount of money circulated within the community, and the level of community engagement and reinvestment. Additionally, we can measure success by looking at how Black-owned businesses influence policy changes, contribute to cultural preservation, and inspire the next generation of entrepreneurs.

Another critical measure of success is the resilience of Black-owned businesses. Are these businesses able to weather economic downturns, adapt to changing market conditions, and continue to provide for their communities? Resilience is a key indicator of long-term sustainability, and it's essential for us to support businesses that are built to last.

Finally, success should be measured by the degree to which Black entrepreneurship leads to greater economic independence and freedom. Are Black-owned businesses able to operate without reliance on outside capital, ownership, or control? Are they creating opportunities for wealth generation that go beyond the immediate business owners and extend to the wider community? These are the questions that the *Financial Ark* must address as it continues to build a pathway to economic freedom for Black people.

Starting a Business: Steps to Success

Identify Your Passion and Market Need:

The first step in starting a business is to identify your passion and align it with a market need. What skills, talents, or interests do you have that can be transformed into a business? Conduct market research to identify gaps in the market that your business can fill.

Develop a Business Plan:

A well-thought-out business plan is essential for success. This document should outline your business goals, target market, competition, marketing strategy, operational plan, and financial projections. A strong business plan not only helps you stay on track but also makes it easier to secure funding from investors, banks, or grants. There are many resources available online that offer free templates and guides for writing a business plan.

Secure Funding:

One of the major challenges for many Black entrepreneurs is access to capital. Traditional banks and investors may have discriminatory lending practices, but there are alternatives. Black-owned banks, credit unions, crowdfunding platforms, and venture capital firms that focus on minority-owned businesses are available options. Additionally, local, or national grants for minority entrepreneurs can provide seed money to help get your business off the ground.

Funding your business through your own savings or earnings from side hustles is also a viable option if outside capital is difficult to obtain. Regardless of the method, ensure you have enough funding to cover startup costs and sustain the business through its initial growth phase.

Establish a Legal Structure:

Choosing the right legal structure for your business is critical. You can operate as a sole proprietor, form a partnership, establish a limited liability company (LLC), or incorporate. Each option has different tax implications, liability protection, and operational requirements. Consult with a legal professional or use online legal services to determine which structure best suits your needs.

Register Your Business and Obtain Licenses:

Once you have decided on a legal structure, you will need to register your business with your state and obtain any necessary licenses and permits. Check with local, state, and federal authorities to ensure your business complies with all regulations.

Build Your Brand:

Branding is a key aspect of a successful business. Develop a strong brand identity that resonates with your target audience. This includes creating a memorable logo, designing a professional website, and establishing a presence on social media platforms relevant to your audience. Consistency in branding will help build recognition and trust among your customers.

Market Your Business:

Use both online and offline marketing strategies to promote your business. Social media, search engine optimization (SEO), and email marketing are cost-effective ways to reach a wide audience. If your budget allows, you can also invest in digital ads or traditional advertising like billboards and flyers. Focus on building relationships with your customers and offering value that keeps them coming back.

Network and Build Partnerships:

Networking is an invaluable tool for growing your business. Attend local business events, join industry associations, and connect with other entrepreneurs. Establishing partnerships with other Black-owned businesses or complementary companies can also open new opportunities for growth and collaboration.

Focus on Customer Service and Continuous Improvement:

Customer satisfaction is the backbone of any successful business. Ensure that your product or service meets the needs of your customers, and always strive to improve. Regularly seek feedback from your clients and adapt your offerings based on their input. Loyal customers are likely to refer others, helping your business grow organically.

Expand and Diversify:

Once your business has gained traction, explore opportunities for expansion. This could mean opening new locations, introducing new products or services, or expanding your market reach through e-commerce. Diversifying your revenue streams will help stabilize your business and protect against market fluctuations.

Resources for Starting a Business

1. **SBA (Small Business Administration)**
    - **What it offers**: The SBA provides free resources, loans, and grants for small businesses. They also offer educational tools, mentorship programs, and step-by-step guides for new entrepreneurs.

- **Best for**: Anyone looking to start or grow a small business in the U.S.
- **Website**: sba.gov
2. **Score**
    - **What it offers**: Score is a nonprofit association offering free mentoring and educational resources for small business owners. They have a network of experienced business mentors who provide guidance in various aspects of entrepreneurship.
    - **Best for**: Aspiring entrepreneurs seeking mentorship and advice.
    - **Website**: score.org
3. **WeWork Labs**
    - **What it offers**: WeWork Labs is an innovative platform offering workspace, mentorship, and networking opportunities. It is ideal for startups in the tech industry or entrepreneurs looking to grow their network.
    - **Best for**: Startups and entrepreneurs looking for coworking spaces and growth programs.
    - **Website**: wework.com
4. **LegalZoom**
    - **What it offers**: LegalZoom provides services for setting up your business structure, such as LLCs, corporations, or partnerships. It also offers legal support, document filing, and trademark assistance.
    - **Best for**: Entrepreneurs who need help with legal documentation and compliance.
    - **Website**: legalzoom.com
5. **Shopify**
    - **What it offers**: Shopify is a platform that helps businesses create and manage online stores. It offers tools for marketing, sales, and inventory management.
    - **Best for**: E-commerce entrepreneurs.
    - **Website**: shopify.com

Other Resources for Starting a Business

- **Kauffman Foundation**
    - **What it offers**: The Kauffman Foundation is focused on entrepreneurship and offers research, data, and resources to help entrepreneurs build successful businesses. It funds programs and initiatives to encourage innovation and business growth.
    - **Best for**: Entrepreneurs seeking data-driven insights and research.

- **Website**: kauffman.org
- **Entrepreneur.com**
    - **What it offers**: Entrepreneur.com provides a wealth of articles, how-to guides, and success stories for aspiring business owners. Their website offers tips for starting, managing, and growing a business.
    - **Best for**: Entrepreneurs looking for general advice, business ideas, and startup news.
    - **Website**: entrepreneur.com
- **HubSpot for Startups**

    What it offers: HubSpot for Startups provides marketing, sales, and customer relationship management (CRM) software, along with educational resources to help small businesses grow. They offer a startup-friendly pricing program to make their software affordable.

    Best for: Tech startups and businesses focusing on digital marketing.

    Website: hubspot.com

- **Black Business Association (BBA)**

What it offers: BBA is one of the oldest organizations dedicated to the growth of Black-owned businesses. It offers advocacy, networking opportunities, and business resources tailored to the needs of Black entrepreneurs.

Best for: Black entrepreneurs looking for support and advocacy.

Website: bbala.org

These platforms and organizations offer a range of support from mentorship to financial resources and educational tools, helping entrepreneurs at all stages of their journey. Whether you need legal advice, funding, or community support, you can find options that suit your specific business needs.

Conclusion: Starting a Business as the First Pillar of the *Financial Ark*

Starting a business is the foundation of the *Financial Ark Philosophy* because it provides Black people with the means to control their economic destiny, create jobs, and build wealth. Through entrepreneurship, Black communities can break free from the limitations of traditional employment structures, address systemic inequalities, and build self-sustaining economies.

But entrepreneurship is not just about financial success; it's about empowerment, resilience, and collective progress. By fostering a culture of entrepreneurship that prioritizes community development, equity, and innovation, the *Financial Ark Philosophy* sets the stage for a future where Black people can achieve true independence, power, and freedom.

As we move forward, the next pillars of the *Financial Ark Philosophy,* investing in the stock market, real estate, and God, will further solidify this foundation, ensuring that Black people have multiple pathways to economic prosperity and security. Together, these pillars will help build a future where Black communities are no longer vulnerable to external economic forces but are instead in full control of their own destinies.

Section Two

Investing in the Stock Market: The Second Pillar of the *Financial Ark*

The second essential plank of the *Financial Ark* is investing in the stock market. While starting a business offers direct control over income and employment, investing in the stock market opens the door to broader wealth-building opportunities. The stock market represents a powerful tool for generating passive income, creating financial security, and gaining ownership in the larger economy. Yet, for many in the Black community, the stock market is viewed as an unfamiliar or inaccessible realm, shrouded in complexity and risk. However, to achieve true economic independence, power, and freedom, Black people should consider embracing the stock market as a critical avenue for wealth creation. *Just as Noah's Ark was a vessel designed to save humanity from an impending disaster, the Financial Ark envisions stock market investment as a way to safeguard against financial insecurity and the unpredictable shifts in the economy that disproportionately affect Black communities.*

By becoming active participants in the stock market, Black individuals and families can benefit from the growth of industries and companies that shape the modern world. More importantly, stock market investments allow for *long-term financial planning* and *generational wealth transfer*, critical components of economic freedom that extend beyond the lifespan of a single business or paycheck.

Overcoming Barriers to Stock Market Participation

Historically, Black Americans have been systematically excluded from many wealth-building opportunities, including access to the stock market. From redlining and discriminatory lending practices to financial literacy gaps and mistrust of financial institutions, there are deep-seated reasons why Black participation in the stock market has been limited. But breaking down these barriers is essential to the vision of the Financial Ark. This pillar is not just about personal financial growth, it is about reclaiming economic space and ensuring that Black communities are active players in the national and global economy.

One of the most significant barriers is a lack of financial literacy. Many people, regardless of race, may feel intimidated by the jargon and complexities of the stock market. Terms like "dividends," "capital gains," "index funds," and "asset allocation" can seem foreign and impenetrable to those who did not grow up learning about investment strategies. For Black communities, where economic resources have historically been scarce, stock market education has often been out of reach, contributing to a cycle of financial exclusion.

The *Financial Ark Philosophy* therefore includes and prioritizes education as a foundational element of stock market participation. This means creating accessible, culturally relevant resources that teach the basics of investing, demystify the process of buying and selling stocks, and promote long-term strategies over short-term speculation. Schools, community organizations, churches, and social media platforms can all play a role in spreading financial literacy and helping Black people build the confidence to invest.

Additionally, it's crucial to address the mistrust that many Black people have toward financial institutions. This mistrust is not unfounded. Black Americans have historically faced discriminatory practices that stripped them of wealth or denied them access to fair financial services. For the Financial Ark to succeed, building trust in the stock market must involve promoting financial institutions that prioritize transparency, fairness, and inclusiveness. Black-owned financial firms, investment platforms, and advisors can play a key role in bridging this trust gap and creating a welcoming environment for new investors.

Diversifying Investments: The Key to Long-Term Wealth

One of the key principles of investing in the stock market is diversification. Unlike starting a business, which requires active management and direct involvement, stock market investing allows individuals to spread their investments across different sectors, companies, and even countries. This diversification is crucial because it reduces risk while increasing the potential for returns. The

Financial Ark promotes diversification as a way to build resilient portfolios that can withstand economic downturns and market volatility.

For Black investors, diversification is especially important given the disproportionate impact that economic recessions and market crashes tend to have on marginalized communities. By investing in a broad range of assets, including stocks, bonds, real estate investment trusts (REITs), and index funds, investors can protect themselves against the risk of losing everything in a market slump.

Index funds, for example, are a popular and effective way to diversify investments. These funds track the performance of a specific index, such as the S&P 500. Rather than betting on the success of a single company, investors are spreading their risk across hundreds of companies, making their portfolio more stable and less vulnerable to market fluctuations.

Furthermore, Black investors should be encouraged to diversify across industries that are poised for growth, such as technology, healthcare, clean energy, and artificial intelligence. These industries represent the future of the global economy, and by investing in them early, Black communities can *position themselves* to benefit from the technological and economic advancements that will shape the 21st century.

The premise of the Financial Ark philosophy is not just to get Black people investing but to ensure that they are investing wisely and strategically. By emphasizing the importance of diversification, the Financial Ark advocates that investors build portfolios that are not only profitable but also sustainable over the long term.

Stock Market Investment as a Tool for Passive Income and Financial Freedom

One of the most powerful aspects of investing in the stock market is the ability to generate *passive income*. Unlike a job which requires constant effort and time, stock market investments can generate income with *little to no active involvement*. This passive income comes in the form of dividends, interest, and capital gains, money that is earned simply by owning shares in profitable companies or funds. For Black communities, passive income is a game-changer because it allows individuals to build wealth without being tied to the labor market, which has historically been exploitative and unequal for Black workers. Passive income also provides financial flexibility, giving people the freedom to pursue other goals, whether that means starting a business, furthering their education, or retiring early.

Dividends offer a reliable source of passive income. Many companies pay dividends to their shareholders as a way of distributing profits, and these payments can be reinvested to purchase more shares, compounding the investor's wealth over time. For example, an investor who owns shares in a company like Coca-Cola or Johnson & Johnson may receive quarterly dividend payments, which can either be withdrawn as income or reinvested to purchase additional shares.

Additionally, *capital gains, the profit earned when an investment is sold for more than its purchase price,* can provide substantial returns for long-term investors. While the stock market can be volatile in the short term, it has historically trended upward over time. This means that investors who buy and hold quality stocks for years or even decades are likely to see significant capital appreciation.

By promoting stock market investment as a tool for generating passive income, the Financial Ark Philosophy encourages Black individuals and families to break free from the constraints of traditional wage labor and move toward financial independence. When passive income exceeds one's living expenses, financial freedom is achieved, giving people the power to live life on their own terms.

Long-Term Investing: Building Generational Wealth

While the allure of short-term gains and day trading often captures media attention, the real power of stock market investing lies in long-term, patient wealth-building. For Black communities, who have been systematically denied the opportunity to accumulate wealth for centuries, long-term investing is a critical strategy for building generational wealth. *Generational wealth refers to the assets, investments, and financial resources that are passed down from one generation to the next.* Historically, Black families in the United States have had far fewer opportunities to build and transfer wealth due to systemic racism, discriminatory housing policies, and wage inequality. However, by investing in the stock market and holding assets for the long term, Black families can create a financial legacy that benefits not just their immediate family but future generations.

One of the most effective ways to build generational wealth through the stock market is by using tax-advantaged accounts such as 401(k)s, IRAs, and 529 college savings plans. These accounts offer significant tax benefits, allowing investments to grow tax-free or tax-deferred over time. By maximizing contributions to these accounts and holding investments for decades, Black investors can accumulate substantial wealth that can be passed down to their children and grandchildren. Moreover, estate planning is an essential part of building generational wealth. Black families must be educated on the importance of *wills, trusts*, and other legal tools that ensure wealth is transferred efficiently and with minimal tax liability. The *Financial Ark Philosophy* advocates the need for proactive financial planning, so that the wealth built through stock market investments is preserved and passed on to future generations.

This focus on long-term investing and generational wealth is critical to the philosophy of the Financial Ark. Economic freedom is not just about individual success; it is about creating a financial foundation that benefits entire families and communities for years to come.

Impact Investing and Economic Justice

As Black communities begin to embrace stock market investing, there is also an opportunity to use investments as a tool for promoting social and economic justice. *Impact investing allows investors to put their money into companies and funds that align with their values*, supporting businesses that prioritize diversity, environmental sustainability, and social responsibility. For the Financial Ark, impact investing is a way to harness the power of the stock market to drive positive change. By investing in companies that are committed to creating equitable and just societies, Black investors can ensure that their wealth-building efforts are aligned with their broader goals of racial and economic justice. This might include *investing in Black-owned companies*, supporting businesses that have strong diversity and inclusion initiatives, or choosing funds that focus on environmental, social, and governance (ESG) criteria. Impact investing allows Black investors to build wealth while also contributing to the creation of a more just and equitable economy. Moreover, impact investing can create a sense of ownership within Black communities. When Black investors own shares in companies that are making a difference in the world, they become stakeholders in the fight for social justice, using their financial power to support causes they care about.

Overcoming the Fear of Risk

A common fear associated with stock market investing is the risk of losing money. This fear is particularly prevalent among Black communities, who have historically faced financial insecurity and may be wary of placing their hard-earned money into the volatile world of stocks. However, while risk is an inherent part of investing, the Financial Ark philosophy promotes strategies that mitigate risk and emphasize long-term stability over short-term speculation. Risk can be managed through diversification, as previously discussed, but it can also be minimized by adopting a disciplined, long-term approach to investing. The stock market will always experience fluctuations, but investors who stay the course and avoid panic selling during downturns are more likely to see their investments grow over time.

Moreover, the Financial Ark philosophy encourages Black investors to start small and gradually increase their investments as they become more comfortable with the stock market. By starting with a manageable amount of money and focusing on building a diversified portfolio, investors can gain confidence and experience without taking on unnecessary risks.

Investing in the Stock Market: Steps to Success

1. **Build Financial Literacy**:
   Before investing in the stock market, it is essential to understand the basics. Learn about key concepts such as stocks, bonds, dividends, capital gains, index funds, and diversification. There are plenty of free online resources, books, and financial blogs that offer accessible information for beginners. Many financial institutions also offer courses on investing.
2. **Set Clear Financial Goals**:
   Determine your investment objectives. Are you investing for long-term

wealth building, retirement, or short-term gains? Understanding your financial goals will help guide your investment strategy and the level of risk you are comfortable taking on.

3. **Start Small with Low-Cost Investments**:
   If you are new to the stock market, start with low-cost, low-risk investments. Exchange-traded funds (ETFs) and index funds are great options for beginners because they offer diversification and typically have lower fees than actively managed funds. You can begin investing with small amounts and gradually increase your contributions as you become more confident.

4. **Open an Investment Account**:
   To invest in the stock market, you will need to open an account with a brokerage firm. Many online platforms allow you to open an account with little to no fees, and some even offer fractional shares, meaning you can invest in high-value stocks like Amazon or Tesla without needing to buy a whole share.

5. **Diversify Your Portfolio**:
   Diversification is key to reducing risk in your portfolio. Avoid putting all your money into one stock or one sector. Instead, spread your investments across different industries, countries, and asset classes (stocks, bonds, REITs, etc.). This will help ensure that if one part of your portfolio performs poorly, other areas may still perform well.

6. **Stay Consistent with Dollar-Cost Averaging**:
   Dollar-cost averaging is an investment strategy that involves regularly investing a fixed amount of money, regardless of market conditions. By consistently investing a set amount, you can reduce the impact of market volatility and build your portfolio steadily over time. This strategy also helps prevent emotional decision-making, such as panic selling during market downturns.

7. **Reinvest Dividends**:
   Many stocks and ETFs pay dividends, which are a portion of a company's profits distributed to shareholders. Rather than cashing out your dividends, reinvest them to purchase more shares. This allows your investment to compound over time, increasing your wealth more quickly.

8. **Monitor and Adjust Your Portfolio**:
   While long-term investing is often more successful than frequent buying and selling, it is still important to review your portfolio regularly. Assess your asset allocation, review company performance, and ensure your investments align with your goals. If necessary, rebalance your portfolio to maintain your desired level of risk and return.

9. **Learn from Mistakes and Stay Informed**:
   Every investor makes mistakes, especially in the beginning. The key is to learn from those mistakes and continue growing your financial knowledge. Stay informed about market trends, new investment opportunities, and economic shifts. Subscribing to financial newsletters or joining investment forums can help you stay updated.
10. **Plan for Retirement with Tax-Advantaged Accounts**:
    One of the most effective ways to invest in the stock market is through tax-advantaged accounts such as a 401(k), IRA, or Roth IRA. These accounts offer significant tax benefits, allowing your investments to grow tax-free or tax deferred. If your employer offers a 401(k) match, take full advantage of it, as it is essentially free money that will help accelerate your retirement savings.

Here's a breakdown of some popular platforms and how they compare:

1. Robinhood

- **How it works**: Robinhood offers commission-free trading for stocks, ETFs, options, and cryptocurrencies. It has a simple, user-friendly interface, making it popular for beginner investors. Robinhood became well-known for its zero-fee model, which made investing more accessible to retail investors.
- **Pros**:
    - No commission fees for trades.
    - Simple, beginner-friendly app interface.
    - Supports fractional shares and cryptocurrency trading.
    - Access to IPOs (Initial Public Offerings) for retail investors.
- **Cons**:
    - Limited research and educational tools compared to other platforms.
    - Revenue model based on "payment for order flow" (PFOF), which has been criticized for potential conflicts of interest.
    - Limited customer support and service options.

- o Restricted trading during high market volatility events (like during the GameStop stock surge).
- **Best for**: Beginners looking for an easy-to-use platform with no trading fees.

2. Webull

- **How it works**: Like Robinhood, Webull offers commission-free trading for stocks, ETFs, options, and cryptocurrency. It caters to intermediate and advanced traders, providing a variety of tools such as advanced charts, indicators, and a virtual trading option to practice.
- **Pros**:
    - o Commission-free stock, ETF, and options trades.
    - o Offers more advanced tools and analytics compared to Robinhood.
    - o Supports cryptocurrency trading.
- **Cons**:
    - o Learning curve for new users due to advanced features.
    - o Cryptocurrency trades require a separate app (Webull Pay).
- **Best for**: Intermediate traders, options traders, and those looking for more detailed research tools.

3. TD Ameritrade

- **How it works**: TD Ameritrade is a more comprehensive platform offering stocks, ETFs, mutual funds, futures, options, and even forex trading. It includes educational resources and detailed research tools, making it suitable for both beginners and experienced traders.
- **Pros**:
    - o No commissions on stocks, ETFs, and options.
    - o Extensive research tools and educational resources.
    - o Access to a wide variety of asset types (including futures and forex).
    - o 24/7 customer service.
- **Cons**:
    - o Options and futures trading fees can be higher than other platforms.
    - o Some users report occasional app performance issues.
- **Best for**: New and experienced investors looking for more comprehensive tools.

Conclusion

- **Robinhood** is best for beginners due to its user-friendly interface and commission-free trades, but it lacks advanced tools and has been criticized for its revenue model and customer service.
- **Webull** is a viable choice for intermediate traders seeking more advanced tools and charting features while still offering commission-free trades.
- **TD Ameritrade** provides a full-featured brokerage with extensive resources, making it ideal for both new and experienced investors who want a comprehensive experience.

Each platform has its own strengths and drawbacks, so your choice will depend on your specific needs, whether you are a beginner, active trader, or long-term investor.

Section Three

Investing in Real Estate: The Third Pillar of the *Financial Ark Philosophy*

The third pillar of the Financial Ark Philosophy is investing in real estate, an asset class that has long been recognized as one of the most reliable ways to build and preserve wealth. Real estate holds a unique position within the framework of economic independence because it provides not only financial security but also control over physical space, something that has been systematically denied to Black communities through discriminatory housing policies and redlining practices. The philosophy of the Financial Ark is to empower Black people to reclaim that control and use real estate as a tool to create generational wealth, provide stability, and foster community development.

Just as Noah's Ark was built to protect humanity from the floodwaters, the *Financial Ark Philosophy* sees real estate as a way to safeguard Black communities from financial instability and the volatility of the broader economy. Investing in property, whether residential, commercial, or land, offers Black families a tangible, long-term asset that appreciates over time, provides rental income, and offers a hedge against inflation. Real estate is not just an investment; it is a means of creating permanent ownership and control over one's environment, ensuring that Black communities can thrive in spaces they own.

The Historical Importance of Real Estate in Wealth Building

Throughout history, real estate has played a critical role in the creation of wealth, particularly in America. Homeownership, in particular, has been the cornerstone of middle-class wealth generation for decades. Yet, Black Americans have been systematically excluded from this opportunity through policies such as redlining, discriminatory lending, and housing segregation. These practices have created a significant wealth gap between Black and white families, as homeownership rates among Black Americans have consistently lagged behind those of other racial groups.

The *Financial Ark Philosophy* advocates the reversal this trend by encouraging Black people to invest in real estate as a means of building long-term wealth. Homeownership, for example, allows individuals and families to accumulate equity over time, providing them with an asset that can be passed down to future generations. In addition, owning property allows Black people to escape the cycle of rent payments, which often provide no long-term financial benefit, and instead, create stability and security within their communities.

Beyond homeownership, real estate offers a variety of investment opportunities that can generate both active and passive income. Whether it's purchasing rental properties, investing in commercial real estate, or acquiring land for development, real estate provides multiple pathways to wealth creation, all of which contribute to the overall mission of the *Financial Ark*.

Overcoming Barriers to Real Estate Investment

Like the stock market, real estate investing has historically been out of reach for many Black Americans due to discriminatory policies, a lack of financial resources, and gaps in financial literacy. The high upfront costs associated with purchasing property, down payments, closing costs, and fees, can be a significant barrier for those who lack access to traditional financing. Moreover, many Black families may be unfamiliar with the complexities of real estate transactions, including mortgages, property taxes, and maintenance costs.

The Financial Ark Philosophy encourages the pursuit of financial education on the basics of real estate investment, such as understanding mortgages, calculating property values, and managing rental properties. Additionally, the Financial Ark emphasizes the importance of partnerships with Black-owned banks and credit unions, which can offer fair and equitable financing options to help Black investors enter the real estate market. Moreover, community-based initiatives can help lower the barrier to entry for real estate investment. For example, cooperative housing models or real estate investment groups allow individuals to pool their resources, collectively purchase properties, and share the profits. These models can make real estate investment more accessible for those who may not have the financial means to invest on their own.

The Power of Homeownership and Residential Real Estate

Homeownership is often seen as the foundation of real estate investment because it provides individuals with both a place to live and a valuable asset that appreciates over time. For Black communities, owning a home is not only a financial investment but also a step toward reclaiming autonomy over their living conditions, particularly in neighborhoods that have been historically neglected or gentrified. One of the key benefits of homeownership is the ability to build equity, which refers to the portion of the home's value that the owner truly owns, after accounting for any outstanding mortgage debt. As homeowners pay down their mortgage, their equity grows, providing them with an asset that can be leveraged for future investments or passed down to their heirs.

In addition to building equity, homeownership offers stability in the face of rising rents and housing costs. When individuals own their homes, they are no longer subject to the whims of landlords or market-driven rent increases, providing a sense of security and predictability. This stability is especially important for Black families, who are often disproportionately affected by housing instability and displacement due to gentrification.

The Financial Ark Philosophy encourages Black individuals and families to prioritize homeownership not just as a personal goal but as a way to contribute to the broader economic empowerment of Black communities. When Black families own their homes, they are better positioned to build wealth, resist displacement, and invest in the long-term development of their neighborhoods.

Rental Properties and Passive Income

For those looking to expand beyond homeownership, rental properties offer an attractive opportunity to generate passive income. By purchasing residential or commercial properties and renting them out, investors can create a steady stream of income that can supplement their earnings or fund additional investments. Rental properties are particularly valuable because they provide ongoing cash flow while also appreciating in value over time.

For Black investors, rental properties represent a powerful tool for wealth building, especially in underserved or undervalued neighborhoods. By purchasing properties in areas with potential for growth and development, investors can benefit from rising property values while providing affordable housing options to their communities.

However, managing rental properties requires careful planning and consideration. Investors must account for maintenance costs, property taxes, and the potential for vacancies. Additionally, rental property management can be time-consuming, requiring a hands-on approach to tenant relations, repairs, and legal compliance. For this reason, the Financial Ark emphasizes the importance of proper education and training for those interested in becoming landlords. This includes understanding landlord-tenant laws, developing strong property management practices, and hiring professionals when necessary to ensure the success of their investments.

Furthermore, rental properties contribute to the broader goal of community development. By providing quality housing options within Black neighborhoods, investors can combat the negative effects of gentrification, which often displaces long-time residents. Instead, they can help stabilize neighborhoods, create local jobs, and ensure that Black communities maintain control over their living spaces.

Commercial Real Estate: Ownership in the Business World

While residential real estate provides security and passive income, commercial real estate represents an opportunity for Black investors to enter the world of business ownership on a larger scale. Commercial properties include office buildings, retail spaces, warehouses, and industrial complexes, all of which generate rental income from businesses that lease the space. Commercial real estate is a powerful investment because it typically offers higher returns than residential properties, albeit with greater risk. Owning commercial property allows investors to participate in the growth of local economies and benefit from the success of businesses that occupy their spaces. It also positions Black investors as landlords and owners in business districts, where they can exert influence over the types of businesses that enter their communities. For example, owning retail space allows Black investors to prioritize leasing to Black-owned businesses, supporting the broader goal of economic empowerment. Similarly, owning office buildings provides opportunities for collaboration with Black entrepreneurs, nonprofit organizations, and community-based initiatives. By investing in commercial real estate, Black investors can create environments that foster Black business growth and economic development.

However, commercial real estate requires a higher level of expertise and financial resources than residential properties. The Financial Ark Philosophy encourages those interested in commercial real estate to seek mentorship, join real estate investment groups, or partner with more experienced investors to minimize risk and increase their chances of success. Commercial real estate can be a challenging but rewarding venture, and with the right strategy, Black investors can use it to build significant wealth and contribute to the economic vitality of their communities.

Land Ownership: A Long-Term Investment

In addition to residential and commercial real estate, land ownership is another powerful way to build wealth. Land is a finite resource, and as populations grow and urban areas expand, the value of land increases. For Black communities, land ownership is particularly significant because it represents a form of control that has been systematically denied to them through centuries of slavery, sharecropping, and discriminatory land policies.

Owning land provides a wide range of opportunities, from agricultural development to real estate development. Investors can choose to hold land as a long-term asset, benefiting from its appreciation, or they can develop it to create housing, commercial properties, or community spaces. For example, landowners might decide to build affordable housing in underserved areas, create community gardens, or develop mixed-use spaces that combine residential, retail, and recreational facilities.

Land ownership also offers Black investors the chance to protect their communities from gentrification. By purchasing and holding land in areas at risk of displacement, Black landowners can ensure that future development serves the needs of the existing community rather than outside developers. This proactive approach to land ownership can help stabilize neighborhoods and preserve the cultural and historical significance of Black communities.

Real Estate Investment Trusts (REITs): A Gateway to Real Estate Investment

For those who may not have the financial means or desire to directly purchase and manage properties, Real Estate Investment Trusts (REITs) provide an accessible entry point to real estate investment. REITs are companies that own, operate, or finance income-producing real estate across various sectors, including residential, commercial, and industrial properties. By purchasing shares in a REIT, investors can gain exposure to the real estate market without the need for substantial amounts of capital or hands-on management. REITs offer the benefits of real estate investment, such as steady income from dividends and long-term capital appreciation, without the complexities of property management.

Investing in Real Estate: Steps to Success

1. **Understand the Real Estate Market**:
   Before jumping into real estate investing, take the time to understand the local real estate market. Learn about property values, rental trends, neighborhood development, and zoning laws. Research areas with growth potential where property values are expected to increase over time.
2. **Assess Your Financial Situation**:
   Real estate investing requires significant upfront capital, so it is essential to evaluate your financial readiness. Check your credit score, save for a down payment (typically 20% for investment properties), and ensure you have enough reserves for property maintenance, repairs, and vacancies.
3. **Choose the Right Type of Real Estate Investment**:
   Decide which type of real estate investment aligns with your financial goals. Options include:
   - **Residential properties**: Single-family homes, multi-family units, or vacation rentals.
   - **Commercial properties**: Office buildings, retail spaces, warehouses, or industrial properties.
   - **Real estate investment trusts (REITs)**: For those who want to invest in real estate without managing properties directly.
   - **Land investment**: Acquiring undeveloped land for future development.

   Start with a type of investment that matches your risk tolerance and financial capacity.

4. **Secure Financing**:
   Most real estate investors do not buy properties outright with cash, so securing financing is a crucial step. Traditional mortgages, hard money loans, or partnerships with other investors can provide the necessary funds. Work with lenders who understand real estate investing and offer favorable terms for investment properties.
5. **Conduct Due Diligence**:
   Before purchasing a property, perform thorough due diligence. This includes a property inspection, reviewing zoning laws, verifying the property's legal status, and assessing potential rental income or appreciation value. Make sure the property aligns with your long-term investment strategy.
6. **Start with Rental Properties**:
   If you're new to real estate investing, starting with rental properties is a

practical way to generate passive income. Renting out single-family homes, duplexes, or small multi-family properties can provide steady cash flow while allowing you to build equity. Screen tenants carefully, and work with a property manager if you don't want to manage day-to-day operations.

7. **Leverage the BRRRR Strategy**:
   The BRRRR strategy (Buy, Rehab, Rent, Refinance, Repeat) is a popular real estate investment method that allows you to scale quickly. By buying undervalued properties, renovating them to increase value, renting them out for steady income, and refinancing to pull out equity, you can use the same capital to invest in more properties.

8. **Consider Commercial Real Estate**:
   For investors with more experience, commercial real estate offers higher returns and longer leases than residential properties. Consider investing in office buildings, retail spaces, or mixed-use properties to diversify your real estate portfolio.

9. **Protect Your Assets and Plan for the Future**:
   Real estate is a long-term investment, so protecting your assets is critical. Set up an LLC or another legal entity to shield yourself from liability. Additionally, have a solid estate plan in place to ensure your real estate holdings are passed on to future generations efficiently and with minimal tax burden.

10. **Use Real Estate as a Tool for Community Development**:
    Real estate investment is not just about personal wealth—it can also be a tool for improving Black communities. Consider purchasing properties in underserved areas, developing affordable housing, or investing in community centers. By using real estate as a force for good, you can contribute to the revitalization and empowerment of your neighborhood while generating returns.

If you are a beginner looking to get started in real estate, there are several platforms, resources, support groups, and organizations designed to help you navigate the industry, educate yourself, and access the necessary tools to make smart investments. Here is a breakdown of some key resources:

Platforms for Getting Started in Real Estate

1. **Roofstock**
   - **What it offers**: Roofstock is an online marketplace for buying and selling single-family rental properties. It offers tools to research, purchase, and manage rental properties, even if you're new to the real estate industry.
   - **Best for**: Beginners interested in investing in rental properties with minimal hands-on involvement.
   - **Website**: roofstock.com
2. **Fundrise**
   - **What it offers**: Fundrise is a real estate investment platform that allows you to invest in real estate without owning physical property. It pools funds from investors to acquire commercial properties and residential real estate projects, offering returns via dividends and property value appreciation.
   - **Best for**: Beginners who want exposure to real estate without purchasing physical properties.
   - **Website**: fundrise.com
3. **Zillow**
   - **What it offers**: Zillow is a popular platform that provides access to millions of real estate listings. It offers tools to help research home prices, rental rates, and neighborhood trends, which can be useful when assessing investment opportunities.
   - **Best for**: Beginners researching property values, neighborhoods, and potential investment opportunities.
   - **Website**: zillow.com
4. **Redfin**
   - **What it offers**: Redfin is a real estate brokerage that offers technology-driven services to help you find properties, connect with agents, and navigate the home-buying process. It also provides data on property value trends and market conditions.
   - **Best for**: Beginners looking to buy or sell property with a more user-friendly experience.
   - **Website**: redfin.com
5. **RealtyMogul**
   - **What it offers**: RealtyMogul is a crowdfunding platform that allows investors to pool resources to invest in commercial real estate projects. It offers REITs (Real Estate Investment Trusts) and private real estate investments with a low initial investment.

- **Best for**: Beginners interested in commercial real estate and passive investing.
- **Website**: realtymogul.com

Educational Resources for Real Estate

1. **BiggerPockets**
   - **What it offers**: BiggerPockets is a popular platform for real estate education, offering forums, blogs, podcasts, and educational resources to help beginners learn about various aspects of real estate investing.
   - **Best for**: Beginners seeking education, networking, and real estate investment advice.
   - **Website**: biggerpockets.com
2. **Udemy**
   - **What it offers**: Udemy offers a variety of real estate courses that cover topics such as rental property investment, house flipping, real estate analysis, and more. Many courses are available at affordable rates and cater to beginners.
   - **Best for**: Self-paced learners interested in structured courses on real estate.
   - **Website**: udemy.com
3. **Coursera**
   - **What it offers**: Coursera partners with universities and institutions to provide real estate-related courses. Subjects range from urban development and property management to finance and investment strategies.
   - **Best for**: Beginners looking for university-level courses in real estate investing and management.
   - **Website**: coursera.org
4. **Khan Academy (Personal Finance)**
   - **What it offers**: While Khan Academy doesn't specialize in real estate, it offers foundational personal finance courses that cover essential concepts such as credit, mortgages, interest rates, and savings. Understanding these basics can help beginners navigate real estate financing.
   - **Best for**: Beginners who need to strengthen their financial literacy before diving into real estate investing.
   - **Website**: khanacademy.org

Support Groups and Networks for Real Estate Investors

1. **REIA (Real Estate Investors Association)**
   - **What it offers**: Local REIA groups offer networking opportunities, workshops, and real estate investment education. Many beginners find value in joining REIA chapters to learn from experienced investors, attend events, and build relationships with real estate professionals.
   - **Best for**: Real estate investors looking for in-person networking, mentorship, and educational events.
   - **Website**: nationalreia.org
2. **Meetup (Real Estate Groups)**
   - **What it offers**: Meetup.com hosts various local real estate investment groups where you can meet other investors, attend events, and learn more about specific areas of real estate. This is a great way to find support and mentorship in your area.
   - **Best for**: Real estate beginners looking to connect with local investors and professionals.
   - **Website**: meetup.com
3. **NAR (National Association of Realtors)**
   - **What it offers**: NAR is a trade association that provides resources for realtors and real estate professionals. While primarily focused on agents, NAR also offers valuable market insights, trends, and educational resources for those interested in the real estate industry.
   - **Best for**: Real estate professionals and beginners looking for industry data and networking opportunities.
   - **Website**: nar.realtor
4. **Women's Real Estate Investors Network (WREIN)**
   - **What it offers**: WREIN is an organization dedicated to supporting and empowering women in real estate. They offer mentorship, education, and a network of like-minded women in the real estate space.
   - **Best for**: Female entrepreneurs and investors looking for community and support.
   - **Website**: womensrein.com

Government Programs and Assistance

1. **HUD (Department of Housing and Urban Development)**
   - **What it offers**: HUD provides information on buying homes, getting mortgages, and government programs that assist first-time homebuyers, especially in low-income areas. HUD also has grant programs for community development and homeownership education.
   - **Best for**: First-time homebuyers and investors seeking affordable housing programs and grants.
   - **Website**: hud.gov
2. **FHA (Federal Housing Administration) Loans**
   - **What it offers**: FHA loans are government-backed loans that are designed to help first-time homebuyers who may not qualify for conventional financing due to low credit scores or limited down payments. FHA loans are a great way for beginners to get started in real estate.
   - **Best for**: First-time homebuyers or investors with low credit or limited savings.
   - **Website**: fha.com
3. **USDA Rural Development Loans**
   - **What it offers**: USDA loans provide affordable financing for homes in eligible rural areas. These loans are great for first-time homebuyers who are willing to invest in properties outside of major urban centers.
   - **Best for**: Buyers interested in rural properties or who need lower down payment options.
   - **Website**: usda.gov

Putting It All Together

When starting in real estate, it's essential to educate yourself, connect with like-minded individuals, and access resources that simplify the process. Platforms like **Roofstock** and **Fundrise** offer entry points for investing in real estate without requiring significant capital or experience. **BiggerPockets** and **REIA** provide the education and networking needed to deepen your understanding of real estate investing. Lastly, using government programs and financial assistance like **FHA loans** can help you get started, even with limited resources.

By leveraging these platforms and resources, you can build a solid foundation for real estate investment, ensuring long-term success in your journey.

Section Four

Investing in God: The fourth Pillar of the *Financial Ark Philosophy*

Incorporating the Pillar of God means understanding that financial abundance is not an end in itself but a means to contribute to the well-being of others, provide for your family, and serve the Kingdom of God. Here are key biblical teachings on money, wealth, and prosperity to guide how the first three pillars are built and sustained.

1. God as the Source of Wealth

The Bible makes it clear that God is the ultimate source of wealth and prosperity. It is God who gives us the ability to generate wealth, not solely through our skills, knowledge, or efforts.

- **Deuteronomy 8:18 (NIV)** – "But remember the Lord your God, for it is He who gives you the ability to produce wealth, and so confirms His covenant, which He swore to your ancestors, as it is today."

This verse teaches that wealth-building is not merely a result of human effort, but it stems from divine blessing and guidance. The talents, resources, and opportunities we have are gifts from God, and it is our responsibility to use them wisely.

2. The Proper Use of Wealth

Scripture encourages us to use wealth not only for our benefit but also to serve others and further God's kingdom. Being good stewards of wealth means using it to uplift others, support the poor, and ensure that material wealth does not overshadow spiritual health.

- **1 Timothy 6:17-19 (NIV)** – "Command those who are rich in this present world not to be arrogant nor to put their hope in wealth, which is so uncertain, but to put their hope in God, who richly provides us with everything for our enjoyment. Command them to do good, to be rich in good deeds, and to be generous and willing to share."

This passage encourages believers to be humble with their wealth, using it to do good deeds, be generous, and help those in need. Prosperity has a purpose beyond personal gratification, it is meant to be shared and to bless others.

3. Seek First the Kingdom of God

A crucial element of the Pillar of God is that our pursuit of financial success must never come before our pursuit of God's Kingdom. Our priorities should be aligned with God's will and commandments.

- **Matthew 6:33 (NIV)** – "But seek first His kingdom and His righteousness, and all these things will be given to you as well."

This scripture reminds us that when we place God first, everything else, including financial security, will follow. Wealth and prosperity should never be idols in our lives but blessings that come as a result of seeking God and walking in His ways.

4. Diligence and Hard Work

The Bible often speaks about the importance of diligence, hard work, and discipline in generating wealth. While God provides the resources, it is our responsibility to use them wisely and work diligently.

- **Proverbs 10:4 (NIV)** – "Lazy hands make for poverty, but diligent hands bring wealth."
- **Proverbs 13:11 (NIV)** – "Dishonest money dwindles away, but whoever gathers money little by little makes it grow."

God expects us to be diligent and hardworking, using the gifts He has given us to build wealth responsibly and ethically. Shortcuts to wealth are discouraged, and sustainable growth through hard work is emphasized.

5. Avoiding the Love of Money

One of the most well-known biblical warnings regarding wealth is the danger of loving money above all else. The love of money can lead to greed, corruption, and spiritual decline.

- **1 Timothy 6:10 (NIV)** – "For the love of money is a root of all kinds of evil. Some people, eager for money, have wandered from the faith and pierced themselves with many griefs."

It is important to distinguish between money as a tool and the unhealthy obsession with it. While wealth is not inherently sinful, placing it above our relationship with God or using it unethically can lead to spiritual harm.

The Call to Action: Applying the Pillar of God

To fully integrate the Pillar of God with the financial pillars, here are some practical steps:

1. **Align Your Financial Goals with God's Will**: Start by seeking God in prayer and asking Him to guide your financial journey. Whether you are starting a business, investing, or buying real estate, ensure your goals align with God's purpose for your life.
2. **Practice Generosity**: Use your wealth to bless others. Tithing, giving to the poor, supporting ministries, and helping those in need are ways to honor God with your financial success (Malachi 3:10).
3. **Maintain Ethical Standards**: Be transparent, honest, and fair in all your financial dealings. Ensure that your business practices, investments, and property dealings are above reproach.
4. **Seek Wisdom and Guidance**: The Bible is rich with principles on wealth, money, and prosperity. In addition to daily prayer, studying scriptures related to finance can offer insight on how to manage wealth according to God's will (James 1:5).
5. **Guard Against Greed and Materialism**: Keep your heart centered on God, not on wealth. Remember that material possessions are temporary, and spiritual wealth lasts forever (Matthew 6:19-21).

By combining the spiritual teachings from God's Word with the practical steps of business ownership, stock market investment, and real estate acquisition, the Financial Ark becomes a powerful means of building generational wealth while staying true to the principles of faith, community, and service. The Pillar of God works in harmony with the other three pillars by providing a spiritual foundation that ensures wealth-building is ethical, responsible, and purposeful.

- **Business Ownership**: Entrepreneurs are called to be ethical leaders, using their businesses to not only generate profit but also to serve their communities and create positive impact. Proverbs 16:3 says, "Commit to the Lord whatever you do, and He will establish your plans."
- **Investing in the Stock Market**: Financial investments should be made wisely and ethically, avoiding greed and speculation. Proverbs 13:22 reminds us that "A good person leaves an inheritance for their children's children," encouraging long-term, responsible investment.
- **Investing in Real Estate**: Real estate can provide not only financial growth but also opportunities for philanthropy, housing for others, and community development. Isaiah 32:18 offers a vision of prosperity, saying, "My people will live in peaceful dwelling places, in secure homes, in undisturbed places of rest."

Creating a Financial Ecosystem

One of the most important aspects of the *Financial Ark Philosophy* is its ability to create a self-sustaining financial ecosystem that benefits not only individuals but entire communities. When Black individuals engage in entrepreneurship, stock market investment, and real estate simultaneously, they create an interlocking system of wealth generation that extends far beyond personal gain.

This financial ecosystem operates in the following ways:

1. **Job Creation and Economic Mobility**:
   By starting businesses, Black entrepreneurs create jobs within their communities, providing employment opportunities for others. This reduces unemployment and underemployment, which disproportionately affects Black communities. As these businesses grow, they contribute to the local economy by providing essential goods and services, supporting other local businesses, and reinvesting profits into the community. The income earned by employees can be used to invest in the stock market and real estate, further expanding wealth-building opportunities within the community.
2. **Wealth Circulation**:
   A key element of economic empowerment is the circulation of wealth within the community. When Black-owned businesses generate income, that money stays within the community rather than flowing out to external

entities. Business owners can use their profits to purchase real estate in Black neighborhoods, supporting community stability and development. Similarly, the wealth generated from stock market investments can be reinvested into local businesses or community development projects, creating a cycle of wealth circulation that benefits everyone involved.

3. **Reducing Economic Dependency**:
The *Financial Ark* empowers Black communities to reduce their dependency on external systems that have historically marginalized them. By owning businesses, investing in the stock market, and controlling real estate, Black individuals and communities gain greater control over their economic future. They are no longer reliant on external corporations, landlords, or financial institutions that may not have their best interests at heart. Instead, they create their own sources of income, wealth, and financial security, leading to greater independence and self-determination.

4. **Building Generational Wealth**:
One of the ultimate goals of the *Financial Ark* is to create a legacy of wealth that can be passed down to future generations. By engaging in all three pillars, business, stock market investment, and real estate, individuals can build a diverse portfolio of assets that can provide financial security for their children and grandchildren. This generational wealth is not just about money; it's about creating opportunities, providing education, and offering a sense of stability and freedom that has historically been denied to Black families.

The Importance of Education and Mentorship

For the *Financial Ark Philosophy* to succeed, education and mentorship are essential components. Financial literacy is the foundation upon which the three pillars rest, and without it, individuals may struggle to navigate the complexities of business ownership, stock market investing, and real estate transactions.

Education must begin at an early age, with financial literacy programs integrated into schools, community centers, and households. By teaching Black children the fundamentals of money management, investing, and entrepreneurship, we can equip them with the skills they need to participate fully in the economy and take advantage of the wealth-building opportunities available to them.

Mentorship is equally important, particularly for those who are new to business, stock market investing, or real estate. Experienced entrepreneurs, investors, and real estate professionals can provide invaluable guidance, helping individuals avoid common pitfalls and make informed decisions. Mentorship also fosters a sense of community and collective progress, ensuring that knowledge and resources are shared among all participants.

Building Financial Institutions That Serve Black Communities

In addition to individual efforts, institutional support is critical to the success of the *Financial Ark*. Black-owned banks, credit unions, investment firms, and real estate development companies play a vital role in providing the financial infrastructure necessary for Black individuals to participate fully in the economy.

These institutions offer fair and equitable access to capital, investment opportunities, and financial services, ensuring that Black people are not subject to discriminatory practices or predatory lending. By supporting Black-owned financial institutions, individuals contribute to the overall health and stability of the Black economy, creating a financial ecosystem that serves the needs of the community.

Final Thoughts: A Call to Action

The *Financial Ark Philosophy* is more than just a financial strategy, it's a Philosophy for Black economic empowerment and freedom. By engaging in entrepreneurship, stock market investing, real estate, and spirituality you can take control of your financial future, build generational wealth, and contribute to the development of Black communities.

Getting started requires action, education, and persistence. No matter where you are on your financial journey, begin today by taking the first step toward one of the four pillars. Whether it's launching a business, opening a brokerage account, or researching real estate opportunities, or enhancing your relationship with God, each step brings you closer to achieving financial independence and creating a legacy that will benefit generations to come.

Now is the time to build independence through the Financial Ark Philosophy. A vessel that will carry you, your family, and your community to a future of prosperity, freedom, and empowerment.

BLACK RISING

"Create the Future"

www.ingramcontent.com/pod-product-compliance
Lightning Source LLC
Chambersburg PA
CBHW081019240526
45471CB00017B/3445